SOCCER STARS OF THE WORLD

AUDREY STEWART

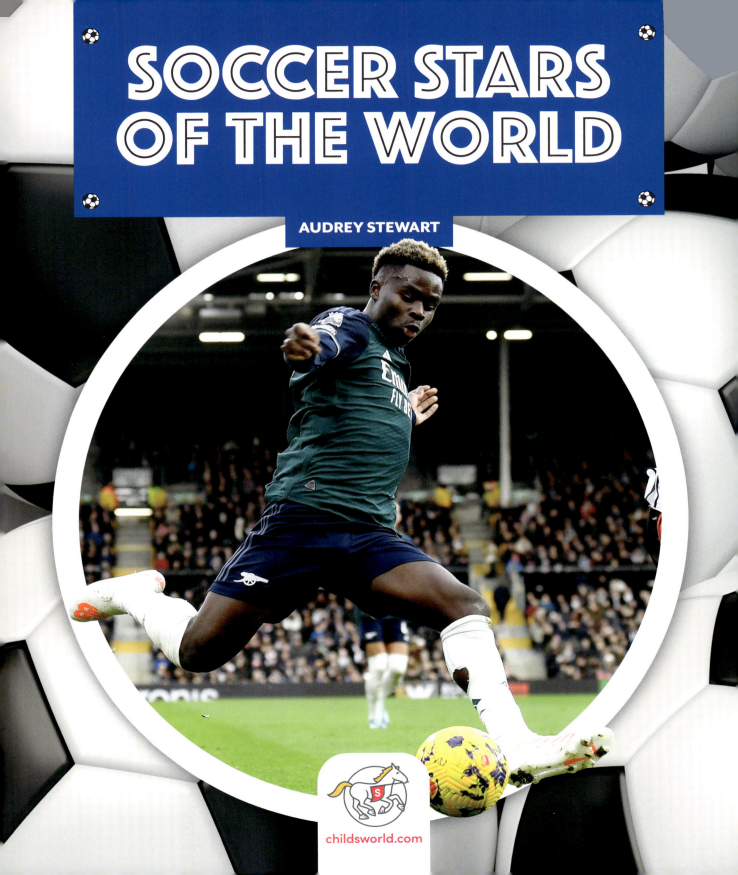

Published by The Child's World®
800-599-READ • childsworld.com

Copyright © 2025 by The Child's World®
All rights reserved. No part of this book may be reproduced or utilized in any form or by any means without written permission from the publisher.

Photography Credits
Cover: © David Price / Getty Images; page 5: ©Mike Hewitt/Getty Images; page 5: ©Andreas Rentz/Getty Images; page 7: ©Pascal Rondeau/Getty Images; page 9: ©David Price/Getty Images; page 10: ©Pedro Castillo/Getty Images; page 10: ©My Life Graphic/Getty Images; page 11: ©Dennis Doyle/Getty Images; page 13: ©Justin Setterfield/Getty Images; page 14: ©Pool/Getty Images; page 17: ©Soobum Im /Getty Images; page 17: ©Eurasia Sport Images/Getty Images; page 18: ©Christopher Furlong/Getty; page 19: ©Angel Martinez/Getty Images; page 21: ©Shaun Botterill/Getty Images; page 22: ©Catherine Steenkeste/Getty Images; page 23: ©Dan Mullan/Getty Images: page 25: ©Elsa—FIFA/Getty Images; page 26: ©Catherine Steenkeste/Getty Images; page 29: ©Michael Regan/Getty Images

ISBN Information
ISBN 9781503894235 (Reinforced Library Binding)
ISBN 9781503895249 (Portable Document Format)
ISBN 9781503896062 (Online Multi-user eBook)
ISBN 9781503896888 (Electronic Publication)

LCCN
2024941436

Printed in the United States of America

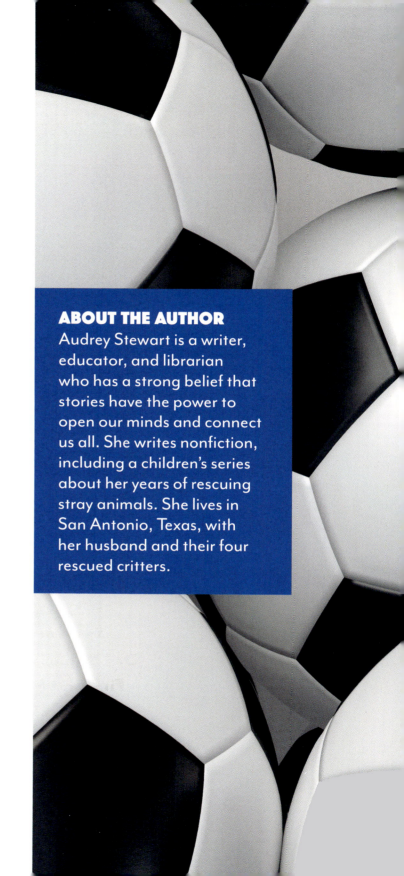

ABOUT THE AUTHOR
Audrey Stewart is a writer, educator, and librarian who has a strong belief that stories have the power to open our minds and connect us all. She writes nonfiction, including a children's series about her years of rescuing stray animals. She lives in San Antonio, Texas, with her husband and their four rescued critters.

CONTENTS

CHAPTER ONE
WHAT MAKES A PLAYER A STAR? 4

CHAPTER TWO
STARS FROM THE UNITED KINGDOM 8

CHAPTER THREE
STARS FROM NORTH AND SOUTH AMERICA 16

CHAPTER FOUR
STARS FROM EUROPE AND AFRICA 20

Glossary . . . 30
Fast Facts . . . 31
One Stride Further . . . 31
Find Out More . . . 32
Index . . . 32

CHAPTER 1
WHAT MAKES A PLAYER A STAR?

Erling Haaland made soccer history in 2023. He scored 36 total goals in the **English Premier League** (EPL) after playing in just 35 matches. Haaland's scoring ability has made him one of soccer's biggest stars in a short period of time.

    Like Haaland, many soccer stars score a lot of goals for their teams. But some stars are defenders and even goalkeepers. So what makes a soccer player a star? It starts with their passion for the game. These players love soccer and have a variety of skills to help make their teams great. Soccer stars respect their coaches. They work together to help their teammates. Star players make smart decisions very quickly to help their team win. The soccer field is big and the ball is moving fast, so soccer stars have to be quick. They have to work together with teammates to be successful. Soccer stars help their teams win titles and trophies by being the best in the game. These players take risks and practice hard. Soccer stars are constantly trying to get better at the game.

WHEN DO PLAYERS BEGIN THEIR CAREERS?

Youth programs are popular around the world. Some are sponsored by schools or community groups. Others are connected to professional **clubs**. The English Premier League has some of the best programs for children in England. These programs are called **academies**, and they have levels for all ages and abilities. Eventually, some players try out for a professional team. Young players might stand out so much that they are asked to move up to the pro level. These soccer stars might start playing with professional teams as young as 13 years old!

Soccer is one of the most exciting sports in the world—and the most popular.

CLUB TEAMS AND NATIONAL TEAMS

Most professional players play for two teams: a club team and their national team. Players typically play for the country where they grew up and have citizenship. Some players have dual citizenship, which means they are citizens of more than one country. They can only play for one country at a time but can switch based on their home country or ancestry. Club teams are a mix of players from everywhere. The team manager finds the best players and makes them an offer to join the club. Sometimes a player suits up for a club game, then flies to another country for a national game the next day!

Haaland grew up playing in Norway, but now he plays for England. The biggest soccer stars come from all over the world. In 2023, Mexico led the way with the most professional players—9,464 pros! Spain, England, and Scotland came in second, third, and fourth place. These players train hard and practice regularly. They are passionate about soccer and make the game a part of their everyday life. Through dedication and commitment, young soccer stars make themselves stand out above the rest. They practice long hours and focus on skill development to be the best. These players train with some of the best coaches in the world. Let's learn more about some of the world's top soccer stars!

More than 250 million people play soccer around the world. In the United States, around 3 million kids are part of a youth team.

CHAPTER TWO
STARS FROM THE UNITED KINGDOM

KATIE MCCABE

Katie McCabe is an Irish left back, forward, and midfielder. McCabe is also the captain of Ireland's women's national team, and she is Ireland's youngest captain in team history. McCabe scored Ireland's first World Cup goal in 2023 with an amazing shot from the corner. She began her career playing on youth boys' teams in Ireland. Her top skills include strength, speed, ball handling, technique, and overall intelligence on the field. A highlight of McCabe's career was winning the **Football Association (FA) Cup** with her club team, Arsenal, for the 2018–19 season. McCabe was the 2023 Arsenal Women's Player of the Season. In April 2023, she won Women's Goal of the Season against Manchester City.

Katie McCabe is one of 11 children. She is the second of her siblings to play professional soccer.

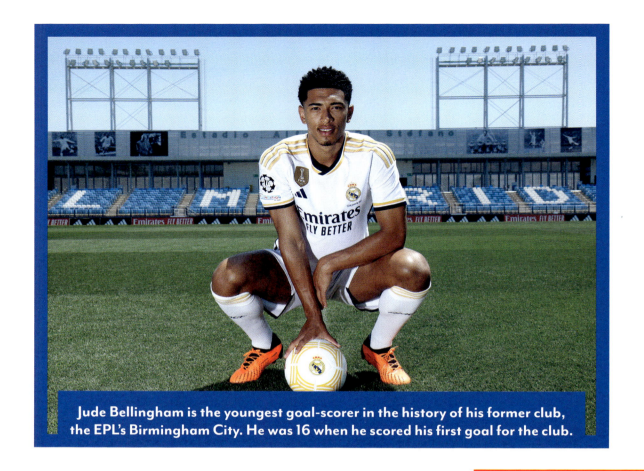

Jude Bellingham is the youngest goal-scorer in the history of his former club, the EPL's Birmingham City. He was 16 when he scored his first goal for the club.

SOCCER POSITIONS

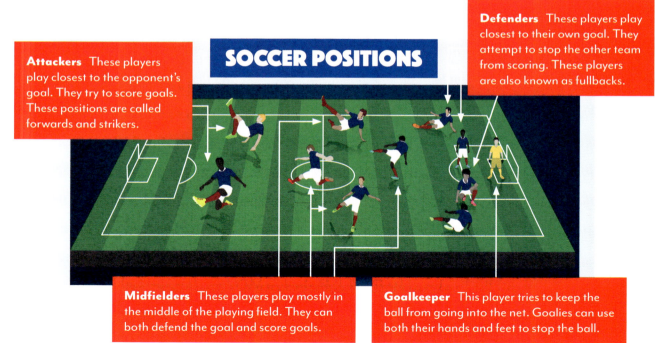

Attackers These players play closest to the opponent's goal. They try to score goals. These positions are called forwards and strikers.

Defenders These players play closest to their own goal. They attempt to stop the other team from scoring. These players are also known as fullbacks.

Midfielders These players play mostly in the middle of the playing field. They can both defend the goal and score goals.

Goalkeeper This player tries to keep the ball from going into the net. Goalies can use both their hands and feet to stop the ball.

JUDE BELLINGHAM

Jude Bellingham is a midfielder for La Liga's Real Madrid in Spain. He also plays for the English national team. Bellingham played for another English team and then played in Germany before joining Real Madrid. He won two big awards in 2023. He won the Kopa Trophy for being one of the best players in the world under age 21. Shortly after, he won the Golden Boy award as the most impressive young European soccer player. Bellingham is great at scoring, but he is also a great defender. He has 35 club goals so far and has scored three goals for England's national team. Bellingham can easily switch from offense to defense to help his team win.

LAUREN JAMES

Lauren James is an English player in the **Women's Super League** (WSL). She plays as a forward. When James was 13, she was **scouted** by the English team Arsenal. Her first appearance with the team was in 2017. James was 16 years old and the second-youngest person ever to play for the team at that time. The following season, in 2018, she joined Manchester United, another English team. She finished that season as their top scorer. In 2021, James joined yet another English team, Chelsea FC, and scored her first WSL **hat trick**. Chelsea won the match 5–1. James is one of the top two scorers for the WSL. She is great at making smart decisions on the field. When James is in a tight corner, she knows what to do to get the ball out and beat her opponents.

Lauren James and two teammates tied as the top scorers for England's national team during the 2023 Women's World Cup.

Bukayo Saka holds the Arsenal FC record for most assists in a season by a teenager. Saka recorded 11 assists during the 2019–20 season.

BUKAYO SAKA

Bukayo Saka plays as a forward for Arsenal FC in the English Premier League. He started playing in the Arsenal Academy when he was eight years old. When he was 17, he joined the senior team. One of Saka's dreams was to score for Arsenal. This dream came to life when he earned the spot as the youngest Arsenal player since 1978 to score 50 goals. One of his nicknames is "Starboy" because of his speed and scoring ability, both with Arsenal and with the English National Team. For both the 2020–21 and 2021–22 seasons, Saka was named Arsenal's Player of the Season. He has fast feet and often beats his opponents down the field. These skills also make him hard to beat when he is dribbling the ball and getting ready to score. Saka is a star because of how fast he moves around his opponents to get the ball in the net.

CHAPTER THREE

STARS FROM NORTH AND SOUTH AMERICA

SOPHIA SMITH

Sophia Smith is a forward for the United States Women's National Team (USWNT). In 2020, the Portland Thorns picked her first overall in the National Women's Soccer League (NWSL) draft. That same year, she made her debut with the USWNT. Smith led the USWNT with 11 goals during the 2022–23 season. She helped her team **qualify** for the 2023 World Cup in a 5–0 win against Jamaica. Smith scored her first World Cup goal when Team USA played Vietnam. Smith has scored 40 goals with her club team in Portland and 16 total goals so far with the USWNT.

LEGENDARY SOCCER STAR: MARTA

Brazilian-Swedish soccer star Marta has been named the **FIFA** World Player six times. She holds the record as Brazil's top international goal-scorer, man or woman, with 115 goals. Marta also holds the record for most goals scored in the World Cup by any player, man or woman, with 17 goals. Marta has great technique, speed, and scoring abilities. She paved the way for young women in sports and went from kicking deflated footballs in Brazil to competing for world titles.

Before she started playing soccer, Sophia Smith played basketball and competed in gymnastics.

LEGENDARY SOCCER STAR: PELÉ

Brazilian player Pelé is considered one of the best soccer players of all time. In his lifetime, he won three World Cup titles with Brazil. When Pelé started out, his family was too poor to buy a soccer ball, so he made one from a sock stuffed with newspaper. He joined a club team called Santos when he was just 15 years old. With fast feet, amazing kicking power, and the instincts to know an opposing player's next move, Pelé stood out on the field. He holds the Guinness World Record for most goals scored in a lifetime—1,279!

VINÍCIUS JÚNIOR

Vinícius Júnior is from Brazil and plays as a forward for Spanish club Real Madrid and the Brazil national team. Júnior began his professional career at just 16 years old. When he was 18, he signed a **contract** with La Liga Club Real Madrid. This decision moved him from Brazil to Spain, where he learned to adapt to a new culture. Júnior played well with his new team and helped them win the Champions League title in 2022. That same year, Júnior debuted in his first World Cup tournament for Brazil. He is known for his speed and dribbling skills. Júnior is a smart player and knows when to make a play that will help his team.

Vinícius Júnior's 2018 contract made him the second-most expensive Brazilian player in the world. He is second only to legendary star Neymar.

CHAPTER FOUR

STARS FROM EUROPE AND AFRICA

ERLING HAALAND

Erling Haaland plays in the English Premier League (EPL). He plays as a forward for Manchester City and for his home country, Norway. He is fast and strong. Haaland stands out on the field at 6 feet, 4 inches tall (193 centimeters) and almost 200 pounds (91 kilograms). Most players his size are defenders, but Haaland is a skilled striker. He holds the record as the youngest player to reach 40 goals in any European league, and he is a top scorer in the EPL. Haaland's dedicated practice started when he was just five years old. He started playing in Norway and continued playing professionally in Austria, Germany, and finally in England. Haaland is considered a star player because of his overall strength and his scoring ability. His team placed first in the league for the 2022–23 season and won the Premier League title for the seventh time.

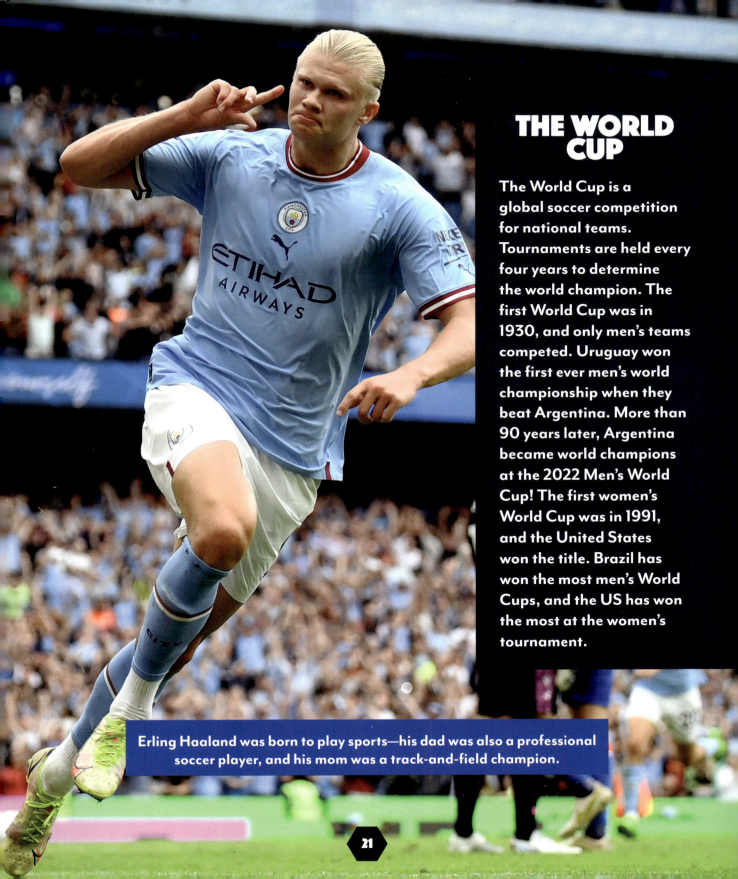

THE WORLD CUP

The World Cup is a global soccer competition for national teams. Tournaments are held every four years to determine the world champion. The first World Cup was in 1930, and only men's teams competed. Uruguay won the first ever men's world championship when they beat Argentina. More than 90 years later, Argentina became world champions at the 2022 Men's World Cup! The first women's World Cup was in 1991, and the United States won the title. Brazil has won the most men's World Cups, and the US has won the most at the women's tournament.

Erling Haaland was born to play sports—his dad was also a professional soccer player, and his mom was a track-and-field champion.

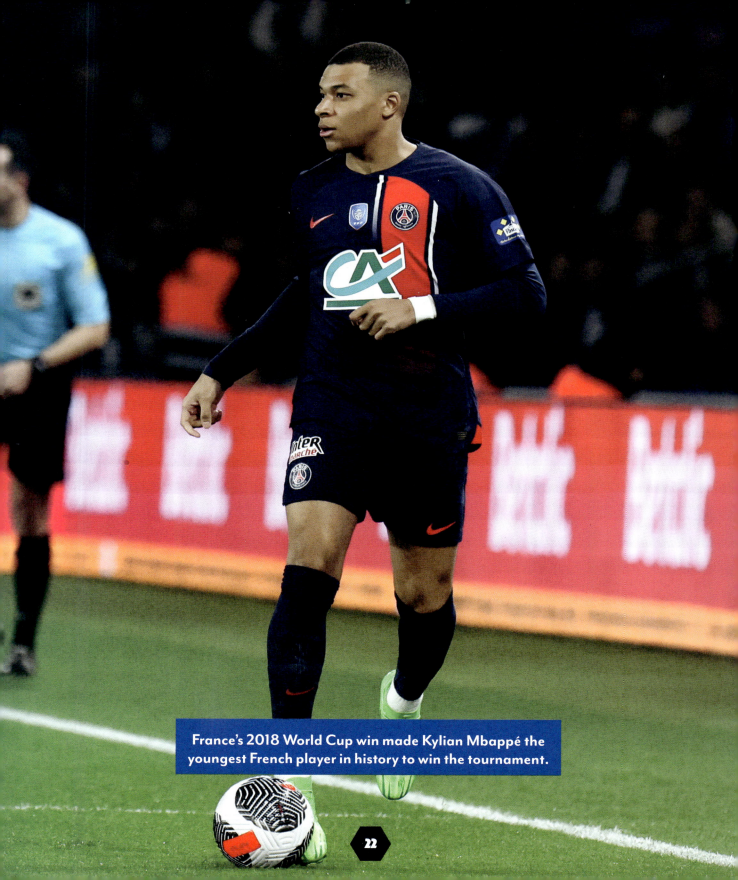

France's 2018 World Cup win made Kylian Mbappé the youngest French player in history to win the tournament.

KYLIAN MBAPPÉ

Kylian Mbappé is a French forward and captain for the France National Team. Mbappé also played for the French club team Paris Saint-Germain (PSG) from 2018–2024. In 2018, he became the youngest French player to score in a World Cup game. France won the World Cup that year. Mbappé won the FIFA World Cup **Golden Boot** award a few years later in 2022, and France placed second behind Argentina. This was his second time on the World Cup stage. For his club team, Mbappé won Player of the Year for the league four times. Mbappé has it all: he can score, dribble, defend, and lead his team to victory.

AITANA BONMATÍ CONCA

Aitana Bonmatí Conca is from Catalonia, Spain. She plays as a midfielder for the Spanish club team Barcelona and for Spain's national team. In 2021, she and her team won the Champions League final. Conca was named Most Valuable Player (MVP) for helping Barcelona beat Chelsea 4–0. She also won Best FIFA Women's Player for 2023. Conca is a great team player and a powerful scorer. She moves the ball and scans the field until she sees an opening to pass or to score. Conca is one of the game's best players because she is quick, clever, and consistent. Her team can rely on her to help them win.

Aitana Bonmatí won the Golden Ball as the best overall player at the 2023 Women's World Cup.

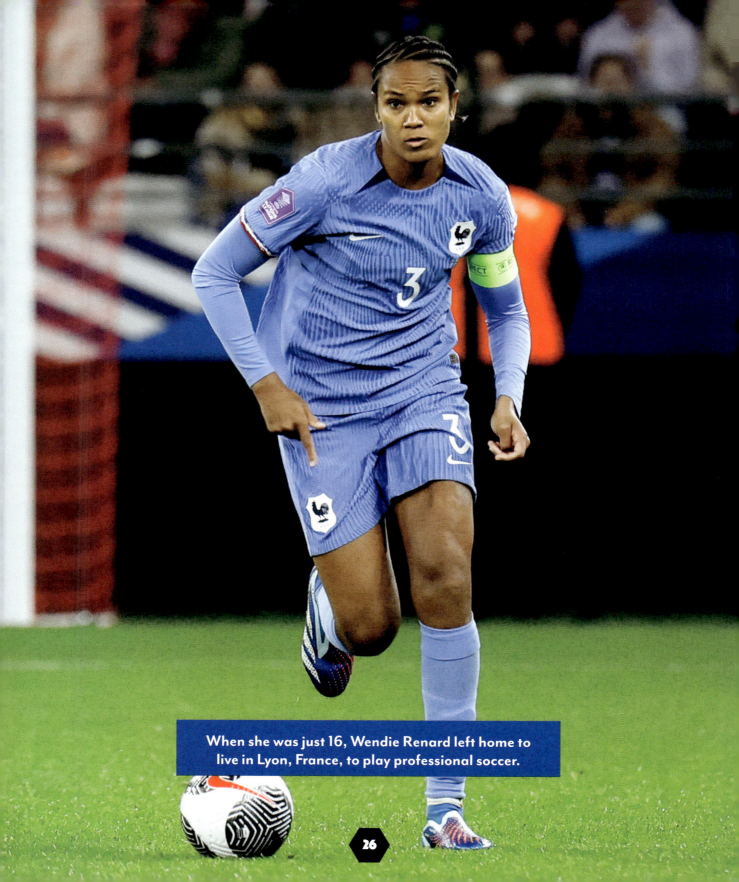

When she was just 16, Wendie Renard left home to live in Lyon, France, to play professional soccer.

WENDIE RENARD

Wendie Renard is a defender for the French club team Lyon. She also plays for the French national team. Renard started playing soccer when she was seven. She joined the professional team Rapid Club Le Lorrain at age 16. Renard is more than 6 feet (183 cm) tall, and one of her best skills is her ability to control the ball with her head. Players will often use their heads to direct a ball that is high in the air. This move helps to pass the ball, direct the ball onto the ground, or score. Renard scored the winning goal with her head during the Champions League semi-final match between Paris Saint-Germain and Lyon in the 2019–20 season. Renard and Lyon went on to win the tournament. Renard's skills have earned her eight European Cup trophies and 14 league titles.

INTERNATIONAL SOCCER'S TOP SCORERS

Player	Country	International Goals
Christine Sinclair	Canada	190
Abby Wambach	USA	184
Mia Hamm	USA	158
Carli Lloyd	USA	134
Maysa Jbarah	Jordan	133
Kristine Lilly	USA	130
Birgit Prinz	Germany	128
Cristiano Ronaldo	Portugal	128
Alex Morgan	USA	121
Julie Fleeting	Scotland	116
Marta	Brazil	115

MOHAMED SALAH

Mohamed Salah is an Egyptian soccer star. He plays as a forward for the English Premier League team Liverpool. Salah is also a captain for his national team in Egypt. He is a high-scoring player and was ranked fourth overall for the 2022–23 Premier League season with 19 goals. Salah won African Footballer of the Year and Premier League Player of the Season in 2017–18. He won the Golden Boot three times for being a top scorer. Salah's dribbling, scoring, and quick thinking on the field contribute to the success of both Liverpool and his national team. Salah helped his national team qualify for the 2018 World Cup after Egypt had failed to qualify for almost 30 years. He is ranked first for scoring on his club team in the 2023–24 season.

Mohamed Salah is the fastest player in Liverpool history to score 50 goals. In his first two seasons with the club, Salah scored 50 goals in just 65 games.

GLOSSARY

academies (uh-KAD-uh-meez) training teams that are connected to larger soccer clubs where players learn the basics of soccer

clubs (KLUBS) professional soccer teams

contract (KON-trakt) a document stating the rules or terms of a business agreement

English Premier League (ENG-lish pruh-MEER LEEG) the highest level of the men's English football league system

FIFA (FEE-fah) short for Fédération Internationale de Football Association; the group that oversees international soccer

Football Association (FA) Cup (FOOT-ball uh-soh-see-AY-shun KUP) an annual knockout football competition in English football

Golden Boot (GOL-dun BOOT) a trophy awarded to the top goal-scorer in a league or at the World Cup

hat trick (HAT TRIK) the scoring of three goals in one game

qualify (KWAL-uh-fy) to have the skill or status required to participate in an event, such as a sports tourment

scouted (SKAUW-tud) searched for talent in a sport

Women's Super League (WEH-munz SOOP-er LEEG) the highest level of the women's English football league system

FAST FACTS

- Brazil leads the way for men's FIFA World Cup titles. They earned five trophies from 1958 to 2002. The US has won the most women's World Cup titles with four.

- Sir Alex Ferguson has 528 wins as a manager in the EPL. He managed Manchester United FC from 1986 to 2013 and is considered one of the most successful managers in history.

- Christine Sinclair has scored the most international goals of all time, with 190.

- FIFA estimates that there are nearly 130,000 professional soccer players worldwide and almost 4,400 club teams.

ONE STRIDE FURTHER

- Research a country and learn more about its national soccer team and professional league. Find out who their top players are and some of the other teams they play. Look on a map to see how close these football clubs are to each other.

- England's Premier League includes many teams in a small area compared to Major League Soccer in the United States. Research these two countries and compare the two leagues and their fan base. How are they similar? How are they different?

- Based on what you learned in this book, what are some of the top skills you would need to be a successful soccer star? What would help you do your best?

- Ask some friends or family members who their favorite soccer star is. Make a chart to see who is the most popular player.

FIND OUT MORE

IN THE LIBRARY

Ashby, Kevin and Michael Part. *Kylian Mbappé the Golden Boy*. Beverly Hills: Sole Books, 2021.

Jökulsson, Illugi. *Stars of Women's Soccer.* New York: Abbeville Press, 2021.

Mugford, Simon and Dan Green. *Soccer Superstars: Soccer Rules the World.* London: Welbeck Children's, 2023.

ON THE WEB

Visit our website for links about soccer stars of the world:

childsworld.com/links

Note to Parents, Caregivers, Teachers, and Librarians: We routinely verify our web links to make sure they are safe and active sites. So encourage your readers to check them out!

INDEX

academy, 15

attacker, 10

club, 5–6, 8, 10–11, 16, 18, 23–24, 27–29

defender, 4, 10–11, 20, 27

English Premier League, 4–5, 15, 20, 28

goalkeeper, 4, 10,

midfielder, 8, 10–11, 24

National Women's Soccer League, 16

World Cup, 8, 13, 16–18, 21–23, 25, 28